Sometimes I Feel...

Rebecca and James McDonald

HOUSE OF LORE

Sometimes I Feel...

Copyright © 2014 by
Rebecca and James McDonald

Requests for permission to make copies of any part of the work should be e-mailed to the following address:
Business@HouseOfLore.net

ISBN: 978-0-9863151-0-7

First House of Lore paperback
edition, 2014

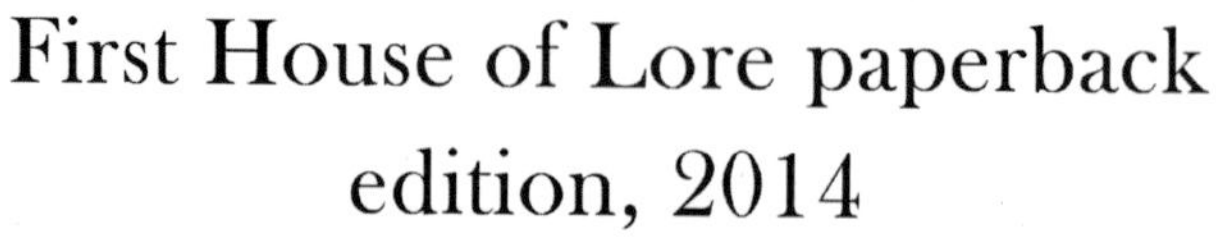

www.HouseOfLore.net

Sometimes I Feel
Happy

Sometimes I Feel

Confused

Sometimes I Feel

Shy

Sometimes I Feel

Caring

Sometimes I Feel
Frustrated

Sometimes I Feel
Sick

Sometimes I Feel
Calm

Sometimes I Feel

Excited

Sometimes I Feel

Skeptical

Sometimes I Feel

Quiet

Sometimes I Feel
Wise

Sometimes I Feel
Scared

Sometimes I Feel
Cool

Sometimes I Feel
Mopey

Sometimes I Feel

Sleepy

Sometimes I Feel
Surprised

Sometimes I Feel
Grumpy

Sometimes I Feel
Unsure

Sometimes I Feel

Crazy

Sometimes I Feel
Bored

Sometimes I Feel
Giggly

Sometimes I Feel

Sad

Sometimes I Feel
Silly

Sometimes I Feel
Smart

Sometimes I Feel

Embarrassed

Sometimes I Feel

Sweet

We all have
these feelings.

How Do You Feel?

See Ya Later!

Checkout
www.HouseOfLore.com
for more children's
books.

Made in the USA
San Bernardino, CA
05 November 2017